Art and Culture of

Ancient Greece

Art and Culture of

Ancient Greece

Dimitra Tsakiridis and Matilde Bardi

rosen publishing's
rosen
central

New York

This edition published in 2010 by:

The Rosen Publishing Group, Inc.
29 East 21st Street
New York, NY 10010

Additional end matter copyright © 2010 by The Rosen Publishing Group, Inc.

Library of Congress Cataloging-in-Publication Data

Tsakiridis, Dimitra.
Art and culture of ancient Greece / Dimitra Tsakiridis and Matilde Bardi.
    p. cm.—(Ancient art and cultures)
Includes bibliographical references and index.
ISBN 978-1-4358-3590-0 (library binding)
ISBN 978-1-61532-883-3 (pbk)
ISBN 978-1-61532-884-0 (6 pack)
1. Greece—History—To 146 B.C.—Juvenile literature. 2. Greece—Civilization—To 146 B.C.—
Juvenile literature. 3. Greece—Social life and customs—Juvenile literature. I. Bardi, Matilde. II. Title.
DF77.T73 2010
938—dc22

                                                                            2009033177

Manufactured in the United States of America

CPSIA Compliance Information: Batch #LW10YA: For Further Information contact Rosen Publishing, New York, New York at 1-800-237-9932

Copyright © McRae Books, Florence, Italy.

Contents

Introduction

The dry, mountainous lands of Greece in the northeastern corner of the Mediterranean were the home of the first great civilization in Europe. The city-states of ancient Greece were located in the same area as the earlier Minoan and Mycenaean civilizations and were influenced by them to a certain extent. However, when Classical Greece reached its peak in the 5th century BCE it was a unique and extraordinary civilization. It was never united into a single political state, but remained divided into hundreds of independent city-states. It was nonetheless united by language and custom.

Reconstruction of part of the Dolphin fresco, painted by Minoan artists in the Palace of Knossos around 1600 BCE. Only a few fragments of the original have survived.

Greek art

Highly skilled Greek craftspeople mastered a wide range of techniques. They made statues in bronze, marble and gold, produced and decorated pottery vases in all shapes and sizes and made beautiful jewelry with gold and other precious metals and stones.

These tiny terracotta statues were made in Boeotia around 2,500 years ago. They were children's toys.

Plate with horses, dating to the 8th century BCE.

The Greek world

This map shows the Greek world around 850 BCE as Greece emerged from the Dark Ages. Although the Greek influence would spread much farther in the following centuries, this area remained the center stage of Greek language and culture until Alexander the Great spread them across the Near East 500 years later.

Greek mythology

The Greeks had many complicated myths that varied from region to region. The Romans adopted most of their gods and myths, and from them they were passed down to Renaissance times and then to the modern world.

Vase showing the twins Castor and Pollux, gods of shipwrecked sailors. The two were inseparable, and, when they died, Zeus transformed them into the Gemini constellation.

GREECE

AEGEAN SEA

- Lesbos
- Phokaia
- Smyrna
- Locris
- Megara
- Athens
- Corinth
- Samos
- Miletos
- Sparta

RHODES

CRETE

Close-up view of a frieze on a cup
showing Greek hoplites in the frenzy of battle. The cup dates to
the 6th century BCE. It was made by Archikles and painted by Glauketes.

Vase painting

Much of what we know about Greek rituals, religion and daily life comes from studying Greek vases that, from the 6th century onward, were decorated with scenes from mythology and life at the time. These vases were exported all over the Greek world, probably in exchange for basic food items, such as grain, olive oil and wine.

The Françoise Vase

This large vase (it stands 2.17 feet or 66 cm tall) was found in an Etruscan grave at Chiusi, Italy. Used as a wine-mixing bowl, it is one of the earliest Athenian vases to show mythological scenes. It has six friezes (rows of decoration) on each side with more than 200 figures acting out the scenes. The main frieze (1), which runs around the whole vase, shows a procession of gods and goddesses in honor of the newlyweds Peleus and Thetis. The top frieze shows the Calydonian boar hunt (2) above the funeral games for Patroklos (3). Each handle shows a gorgon (4), Artemis with animals (5) and Ajax carrying the dead body of Achilles (6).

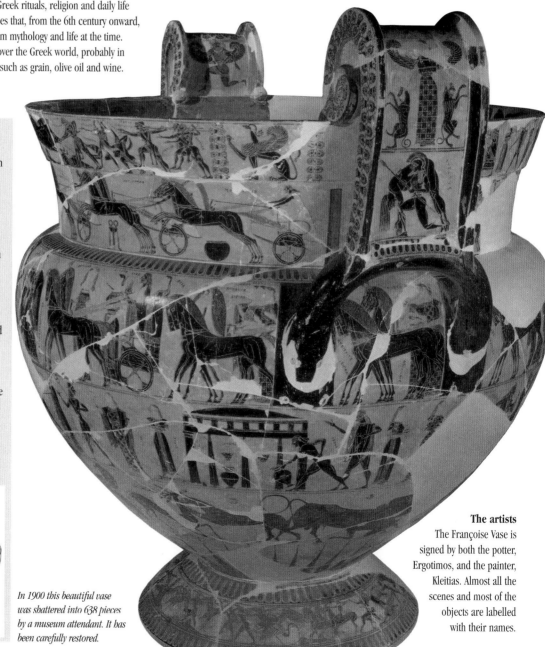

In 1900 this beautiful vase was shattered into 638 pieces by a museum attendant. It has been carefully restored.

The artists

The Françoise Vase is signed by both the potter, Ergotimos, and the painter, Kleitias. Almost all the scenes and most of the objects are labelled with their names.

Minoans and Mycenaeans

Two major civilizations flourished on the Greek mainland and islands before the appearance of Classical Greece. The earliest, known as the Minoan civilization, after the legendary King Minos, dawned around 2700 BCE. It was based on the Mediterranean island of Crete and lasted until about 1450 BCE, when it was destroyed by a combination of natural disaster and conquerors from the mainland. However, many of the great palace cities were soon rebuilt by the Mycenaeans, who also came from the mainland (and were probably the same people who had overrun the peace-loving Minoans). Mycenaean culture absorbed much from its forerunners, although it was never as lighthearted or beautiful. The wealthy Mycenaeans lived in heavily fortified hilltop towns. Their civilization died out during the 12th century BCE, when it was either overrun by conquerors from the north or destroyed by civil war.

Gold face mask from the royal tombs at Mycenae.

Mycenae

Mycenae was one of the largest Mycenaean cities (and gives its name to the civilization). According to legend, it was the capital of Agamemnon, the famous king who sacked the city of Troy. Archaeologists have uncovered large areas of the walled city, including the graves of its wealthiest citizens. These contained masks, pottery, jewelry and other items of great beauty and value.

Skilled Minoan craftspeople produced beautiful objects in the palace workshops. They specialized in luxury items like the rhyton (vase) shown here. This was carved from a single piece of rock crystal. The handle is made from beads carved from rock crystal.

Minoan palaces

The Minoans built huge palaces on Crete, at Knossos (reconstruction shown left), Phaistos, Mallia and in several other locations. The Knossos palace, covering around 2 acres (0.01 sq km), was the largest of them all. Built on several levels, it was arranged around a rectangular courtyard where religious ceremonies were held. The upper floors were luxurious living quarters, while the rooms below served as workshops, warehouses and servants rooms.

This bronze blade showing a dramatic Mycenaean lion hunt is decorated with inlays of gold, silver and black stone.

This gaming board, found at the palace of Knossos, Crete, was made by Minoan craftspeople. It is made of ivory, rock crystal, gold, silver and blue glass paste. Players probably rolled dice to play a game that was somewhere between modern backgammon and chess.

Mycenaean craftspeople produced beautiful pottery. Some pots had geometric designs while others showed animals or people. The distinctive style spread to islands in the eastern Mediterranean where it lingered even after the end of Mycenaean civilization.

Minoan sarcophagus showing a religious ceremony

The sarcophagus (coffin), found at Haghia Triada on Crete and dating to around 1450 BCE, is decorated with two frescoes of religious ceremonies (probably a funeral). On the left, it shows three women marching to the sound of the lyre (1). The woman on the far left (2), probably a priestess, is pouring liquid into a large vase (3). On the right, three men are carrying animals (4) and other offerings toward a figure, probably the person who died (5). The hairstyles (6) and clothing (7) of both the men and the women are typically Minoan in style.

A warlike people

The tombs of Mycenaean nobles have revealed an amazing array of bronze weaponry. Single tombs sometimes contained a dozen richly decorated swords and daggers along with a selection of knives, arrowheads and spearheads. The sturdy bronze suit of armor and helmet made from the tusks of 40 wild boars (above) would have belonged to a wealthy warrior.

The Archaic Period

The time between the end of Mycenaean civilization and the rise of Classical Greece in the 5th century BCE is known as the Archaic period. Little is known of early Archaic times (12th–11th centuries BCE) when the art of writing was lost and the population declined, and this period is called the "Dark Ages." Beginning in about 1000 BCE, many people migrated from the Greek mainland to Asia Minor (now western Turkey) and the Aegean islands in search of better farmland. A northern people, known as the Dorians, settled in mainland Greece at this time. Then, during the 10th-century BCE, conditions gradually improved as population increased and new towns and cities were founded. These small, independent communities were the forerunners of the unique city-states of late Archaic and Classical times.

Two examples of early Greek jewelry. The earring at the top, found in an 8th-century BCE tomb at Athens, has intricate gold decorations. The earring on the left, in gold, was also found in a tomb in Athens. It dates to the mid-9th century BCE.

This vase, dating to the 10th century BCE, is one of the earliest of its kind. Greek vases at this time were decorated with abstract patterns rather than with human or animal figures. This pottery is known as "protogeometric."

The Dark Ages

Some light was shed on the Dark Ages in the 1980s when archaeologists discovered some very rich cemeteries at Lefkandi, on the island of Euboea. They found evidence of a bronze foundry and of trade with Cyprus, Egypt and Palestine dating to around 1000 BCE. They also uncovered a large aisled building made of mudbrick resting on stone foundations. These finds suggest that, at least in one corner of Greece, the Dark Ages were not as backward as was once believed.

Statue of a bard (a traveling musician and storyteller), from the 8th century BCE.

A terracotta centaur (half man, half horse) found at Lefkandi.

Population movements

As the Mycenaean world drew to a close there appear to have been quite large movements of people in various parts of the Aegean. Small waves of migration continued throughout the Dark Ages and the period was generally one of unsettled movement. At this time a people known as the Dorians appeared in mainland Greece and were said to have come from the north. Speakers of the "Dorian dialect" were greeted with hostility from other groups, such as the Ionians (whose most famous city was Athens), whom they would not even allow into their temples.

This painted clay model of a linen chest is decorated with five beehive-shaped granaries with trap doors. It is painted in the geometric style and was found at the site of a 9th century BCE cremation.

Detail of the mourning scene on the Dipylon ampora.

Pottery styles

As population increased and gradual economic recovery began in the 10th century BCE, the growing towns started to produce vases with a new decorative style. This time (10th–8th centuries BCE) is known as the Geometric period. Geometric vases were painted with intricate, abstract patterns and some animal or human figures. The patterns were usually highly symmetrical. As trade increased during the 7th century BCE, a flurry of goods were imported from the Near East. They made a huge impact on Greek artists who adopted many Near Eastern motifs, such as animal friezes, incorporating them into their existing style. Known as the Orientalizing style, it led to the development of the "black figure" technique. The subsequent "red figure" technique began in Athens in the 6th century BCE.

Two big vases from the Orientalizing period. One (above) has a mouth in the shape of a griffin's head, a motif typical of the Near East. The other (left), in the shape of a large jug, is decorated with rows of wild goats and other, imaginary animals.

The Dipylon amphora (jar)

The Dipylon amphora is one of the largest and most beautiful of all the geometric vases. Standing over 5 feet (1.52 m) tall, it was originally placed over a woman's tomb as a grave marker. The main scene (1) shows the dead person lying on a funeral bed (2). There are four mourners beneath the bed (3) and seven more on either side (4). The mourners' arms are all raised above their heads in grief. The neck of the vase has a row of antelopes (5) near the top.

City-states

By about 750 BCE almost all of Greece was divided into independent, self-governing communities known as city-states. A city-state, or *polis*, as the Greeks called it, was not like a modern city. The term refers to a community of people living in a town and the surrounding countryside who were bound together by a common legal and judicial system and also by a common spirit and shared mythology and religious beliefs. At first the city-states were dominated by aristocratic families and military leaders, but as time went on many of them developed more democratic forms of government. In some, male citizens were elected and they met to discuss how the city-state should be run.

The several hundred city-states in Greece were quite similar in form. Each one was centered on a town, with protective walls(1) around it. There was usually an acropolis (2) on a hill in the center and an agora (3) nearby. Most were situated on a river (4) or near the sea (5) to facilitate transportation and trade.

Homer

Almost nothing is known about the life and background of the Greek poet Homer, author of the *Iliad* and the *Odyssey*. However, most scholars agree that he composed the poems (he may not have written them down; this may have been done after his death) during the 9th or 8th century BCE. Homer's poems were very important to the ancient Greeks; they were the basis of Greek education and culture and well-educated people knew large parts of them by heart. They were valued as a symbol of Greek unity and a source of moral and practical guidance. The poems have been translated into many different languages and have continued to fascinate readers ever since.

A terracotta vase from Mykonos with an almost cartoon-like depiction of the Trojan horse episode from Homer's Iliad.

The Trojan horse

During the Orientalizing period Greek artists began to use themes from literature to decorate their vases. The Trojan horse scene above illustrates the well-known episode in the *Iliad* when the Greeks trick the Trojans into dragging a wooden horse filled with warriors inside the city walls. When the Trojans go to sleep that night the soldiers come out of the horse. Catching their enemies unawares, they are able to take the city and win the war. The scene is carved into the neck of a clay vase made in about 650 BCE. It shows the horse (1) on wheels (2). Some of the Greeks are already outside the horse (3), while others are visible inside (4).

Both the Minoan and Mycenaean civilizations had written scripts. With the fall of the Mycenaeans, writing disappeared in Greece. This clay tablet is incised in the Mycenaean script, called Linear B. Scholars have decoded this script, which they recognize as an early form of Greek. The Minoans' Linear A script has not been deciphered. It is not a Greek language.

Archaic sculpture

Large stone statues and reliefs were not produced in Greece before around 680 BCE. Before then statues were smaller in size and mostly carved in wood. Following contact with the Egyptians, the Greeks began to carve in stone. They worked mainly in limestone and marble because this was what they had available. The earliest statues were quite rigid but by late-Archaic times they had become more natural-looking and the anatomy of the human body was better understood. Archaic statues, even the last ones, are all marked by the distance they establish with the viewer. This lends them a peacefulness that places them among the most appealing of all Greek sculpture.

This beautiful terracotta statue of the Greek goddess of fertility, Demeter, was made in a colony in Sicily (Italy). It dates to the late Archaic style and already shows a less rigid body posture.

Archaic statues were generally not very expressive, except for a sometimes strained, sometimes mysterious smile that was the fashion in the first half of the 6th century.

This small limestone statue, known as the Goddess of Auxerre, *is a typical example of an early Archaic statue. She is standing in a rigid pose and wearing a thick layered wig. It was made in Crete in the mid-7th century BCE.*

Right: The head of a famous statue, known as the Rampin Horseman. Dating to the mid-6th century BCE, it was placed in the Acropolis in Athens. The elaborate, tightly curled hairstyle is typical of statues in the late-Archaic style.

Although most of the Archaic statues have now lost their colors, originally they were all brightly painted. Traces of coloring are still visible on many, as on this kore *(girl) from Athens, sculpted in around 510 BCE.*

Terracotta head of a warrior, made in Rhodes in the 6th century BCE. Many of these tiny figures were produced in a range of shapes; they were used to hold perfume.

This reconstruction of a sculptor at work is based on a painting on a Greek vase.

Religion and the Gods

Although the Greeks did not have a special word for religion, this doesn't mean that they had no gods or religious beliefs. On the contrary, they believed in many gods and goddesses and religion entered into most aspects of their daily lives. The 12 most important gods and goddesses, most of whom were Zeus's brothers, sisters or children, were believed to live in a sprawling palace on Mount Olympus. There was also another group of gods, gathered around the figure of Hades, god of the Underworld. These deities were believed to live inside the earth. Every village and town was dedicated to a god or goddess who was worshiped on a regular basis. Almost every group—like a family or town— was considered a religious unit, and everything—like sporting events, feast days, weddings and funerals—was a religious event.

The oracle of Apollo at Adelphi was the most important one for the Greeks. People came from all over the ancient world to consult it.

The Olympian gods and goddesses

ZEUS: the chief god, and the god of justice; ***HERA:*** the jealous wife of Zeus, she was worshiped throughout Greece; ***APOLLO:*** a powerful, widely worshiped god of religious law and the foundation of cities. He was also the god of music, poetry and dance; ***ARTEMIS:*** goddess of the hunt, nature, chastity and childbirth; ***ATHENA:*** goddess of war and crafts. She was the patron goddess of the city of Athens; ***ARES:*** a god of war and the spirit of battle; ***APHRODITE:*** goddess of love and beauty; ***DEMETER:*** goddess of grain and "Mother Earth"; ***HEPHAESTUS:*** blacksmith god of fire; ***POSEIDON:*** god of the sea, earthquakes and horses; ***HERMES:*** a fertility god. The messenger of the gods and the carrier of souls to the Underworld, also the god of shepherds; ***HESTIA:*** goddess of the home and family.

Right: Classical statue of beautiful Artemis, the goddess of wild animals and plants, the hunt, chastity and childbirth. She was the daughter of Zeus and Leto, and the twin sister of Apollo. Artemis was probably based on much earlier nature goddesses. Young Greek women danced in the woods in her honor. The goddess herself was believed to dance in the mountains, streams and wooded groves. She was the favorite goddess of country people.

This 5th-century statue from Olympia shows the chief god Zeus carrying the boy Ganymede off to be his cupbearer on Mount Olympus.

This statue shows the goddess of love, Aphrodite, as the goat-footed satyr Pan tries to embrace her. The goddess has removed a sandal with which she is playfully threatening to strike him. A little Eros hovers above the goddess's shoulder and has seized hold of one of Pan's horns.

Sanctuaries and oracles

Sanctuaries were important places of worship. They were dedicated to a god or goddess in gratitude for a fortunate event, such as winning a war, or surviving a famine or plague. Some sanctuaries had temples, gates and walls; others were simply marked out on the ground with a row of stones. There were hundreds of sanctuaries throughout Greece. Many sanctuaries also had oracles that people came to consult to find out about the future. Most important decisions, such as whom to marry, were only made after seeking the advice of an oracle. Even important questions of state, including whether to go to war, all required an oracular consultation.

According to legend, Delphi was the center of the world. The Greeks built a large stone monument, known as "the navel of the world" to celebrate this. A copy of the original is stored in the Delphi museum.

This red figure vase (right) shows the gods Poseidon, Ares and Hermes fighting against four giants. It probably refers to the Battle of the Giants myth, according to which Mother Earth gave birth to the fearsome giants to punish Zeus. As soon as the giants were born they attacked Olympus, hurling lighted torches, boulders and flaming trees, forcing the Olympian gods to go to war. To be killed, the giants had to be attacked at the same time by a god and a mortal. The battle went on for a very long time, and would never have ended had not the mortal hero Herakles joined in.

Mythology

Ancient Greek poets and playwrights left a rich store of myths and legends about their gods, goddesses and heroes. After Homer, authors such as Hesiod, Pindar, Aeschylus, Sophocles and Euripides, to name a few, recorded or composed works about Greek religion, creation stories, the activities of the gods, stories of human adventures and battle, and many others. These myths inspired Greek artists, and many of their statues and vase paintings show mythological episodes. The myths that were preserved have inspired poets and artists of European descent ever since.

Herakles leads Cerberus to Eurystheus

One of the best-known Greek legends tells of the 12 labors of Herakles. These were set for him by King Eurystheus. This vase painting shows the last labor, in which Herakles (1) brings Eurystheus the ferocious guard dog of Hades (the Underworld), called Cerberus (2). Cerberus had three heads and fearsome snakes rearing up off his muzzles and legs (3). With the help of the gods Athena and Hermes, Herakles was able to enter the Underworld and leave again with the dog (although he first had to wrestle with him). When Herakles arrived at the king's palace with Cerberus, Eurystheus was so frightened that he hid in a large jar (4). Afterward Herakles took the dog back to Hades.

This scene shows the return of the god Hephaestus to Olympus. Born lame, Hephaestus was expelled from Olympus as a youth, either by his mother Hera, or father, Zeus. Here he is shown with the clawed feet of an animal.

This relief carving shows a priest and a priestess standing in front of an inscribed column with their arms raised in a typical gesture of prayer.

Priests and priestesses

As a general rule, male gods were tended by priests and female goddesses by priestesses. Their duties included supervising rituals, punishing people who broke sanctuary rules, and keeping the buildings in good order. Since most sanctuaries were only open a few days each year, priests and priestesses were not particularly busy or important.

Feast days and holidays

Greek religion was not usually a somber affair, and the ancient calendar was punctuated with many feast days and festivals. The most important were annual festivals held to celebrate agricultural seasons or events, usually at sowing time, less often at harvest. Other feast days celebrated rites of passage, such as the registry of newly married brides in their city or village quarter. Family ceremonies were held five days after the birth of a child, to welcome it into the household. There were also festivals to commemorate the dead, especially soldiers who had died in war.

Reconstruction of the procession during the Panathenaia (All-Athens festival). This festival was celebrated with special pomp once every fourth year when the Athenians brought a new woollen gown for the cult statue of Athena in the Parthenon.

A libation, the pouring of a liquid (wine, honey, olive oil, milk or water, or a mixture of these) on to an altar or fire, was another way of honoring the gods or the dead. The man below is holding an olive branch as he performs the libation.

Processions were common in Greek festivals. Sometimes a small group, such as a family, took part, and sometimes, as in the Panathenaic festival held at Athens every year, the whole population paraded through the streets carrying gifts to the temple to offer the patron god or goddess of the city.

Sacrifices and offerings

Sacrifice was an important form of worship. Usually the victim was an animal, although other gifts, such as cakes or fruit, were also common. In a typical animal sacrifice, the thigh-bones of the sacrificial animal were wrapped in fat and burnt on the altar. The rest of the meat was cooked and eaten by the participants during a banquet that followed the sacrifice. Gifts to the gods were made on a regular basis and the gods were expected to receive a portion of the first harvest fruits, libations at drinking parties and a share of the catch from hunting trips.

Tiled roof, with a wooden framework.

The temples all had columns running along the front and sides. Three types of column were used, named according to where they came from. The sober Doric style was the earliest. The Ionian developed in Anatolia, while the ornate Corinthian came from Corinth, in central Greece.

DORIC CAPITAL

IONIC CAPITAL

CORINTHIAN CAPITAL

The statue of the god or goddess to whom the temple was dedicated stood in the cella or naos, and it was here that the priests performed rituals.

The pediment was usually decorated with statues.

This temple has fluted Doric columns with bulges in the middle.

This scene shows a lamb being led to the altar for sacrifice. It was found in the Pitsa cave at Corinth. Dating to over 2,500 years ago, it is very well preserved, even though it was painted on wood.

Temples

Temples were built inside sanctuaries, although not all sanctuaries had temples. The earliest temples, built during the 10th to 8th centuries BCE, were simple wooden huts. These became more elaborate stone structures as the Greeks became richer and their architects more skilled. Temples always faced East–West in alignment with the sun. The altar was situated outside the temple, generally in front of it, presumably so that rituals could be performed in the open air where everyone could see them and take part.

Painted clay model of an early temple. Made in Argos in around 680 BCE, it was dedicated to the goddess Hera.

Classical Athens

Athens was one of the largest and most powerful of the city-states. At its peak in the middle of the 5th century BCE, it was a brilliant center of learning, art and theater. It was also a pioneer in the areas of law and government. By this time all citizens had political rights and the People's Assembly and the popular courts were the main decision-makers. It was a democratic system, although it is important to remember that only men who had been born in Athens were considered "citizens." Women, foreigners and slaves (who made up the vast majority of the population) were excluded.

The statesman Solon was elected archon (chief magistrate) of Athens in 594 BCE. He and one of his successors, Cleisthenes, passed laws that laid the framework for a more democratic society. Solon declared, "The laws I passed were the same for rich and poor. My aim was to obtain justice for all."

In the Archaic period Athens was governed by the city's aristocratic families. During the 6th century BCE they were replaced by tyrannies. The vase painting above left shows the assassination of the Hipparchus, tyrant of Athens, in 514 BCE.

Pericles

Athens reached its zenith under the statesman and general Pericles (c. 495–429 BCE). A highly educated man with broad political views, Pericles was responsible for rebuilding the city, which had been badly damaged during the sack of Athens by the Persians in 480 BCE. He rebuilt the agora, improved the city's roads and enlarged the port of Piraeus. But his greatest undertaking was the construction of the Parthenon and the other buildings on the Acropolis. He also introduced far-reaching political reforms that gave more power to the poorer and less well-connected citizens.

Head of Pericles, wearing a war helmet pulled up on his head.

Pieces of pottery and ostraca, like the ones shown below, were used to record the names of people who, by popular vote, were expelled from the city-state.

The two wheels (below) are public ballots. They were used by voters to convict or acquit someone on trial. Wheels with solid axles, like these ones, were used to acquit the defendant.

Vase painting showing the citizens of Athens voting.

The Acropolis in Athens

The main temples and civic buildings of Athens were all on the Acropolis. This model shows the Acropolis in the 5th century BCE when it was rebuilt after the Persian Wars. The Parthenon (1) was the main temple. On the left stood the Erechtheum (2), a beautiful Ionic temple dedicated to Athena. Next to it was the House of the Arrephoroi (3), where four young girls of noble birth lived. They wove a new *peplos* (gown) for Athena once every four years and performed rituals in her honor. A colossal bronze statue of Athena (4) in military dress stood behind the monumental entrance to the acropolis, which was called the Propylaea (5). To the right was the Temple of Athena Nike (6), the goddess of victory. Behind it lay the Sanctuary of the bear goddess, Artemis Brauronia (7).

Gold statue of Athena, patron goddess of Athens, which stood in the Parthenon, the main temple on the Athenian Acropolis .

Statue of a woman grinding grain into flour. Bread was a staple food in the Greek diet and for many women grinding grain into flour and bread-making would have been daily chores. In large cities like Athens, bakeries were common and people could buy their bread ready-made.

Women were responsible for spinning wool into cloth and then weaving it into garments.

Household furniture was very simple, even in wealthy homes. Many pieces, such as couches, were used during the day for meals and at night for sleeping. This woman (right) is placing some carefully folded linen away in a chest.

Women in Athens

Athenian women had few rights; they could not own property or gain protection from the law, nor could they take part in public life. Their lives revolved around their families. They cared for their husbands and children, ensuring that the household ran smoothly and that everyone had food, clothing and other daily necessities. In some ways poor women may have been better off than wealthy ones; at least they could leave the house to go shopping or work without a chaperone.

Foreigners

Like all large cities Athens attracted many foreigners. Some were freed slaves, but many others were merchants, traders and intellectuals. Even the wealthiest of them had no political rights. Pericles passed a law making citizenship even stricter: both parents had to be born in the city.

This scene from the inside of an Athenian cup of around 430 BCE shows a reading lesson. The boy is reading from a folded wooden tablet, while the man reads from a scroll.

Archaic statue of a sphinx from the Acropolis. The sphinx was a typically eastern image that the Greeks adopted.

Education

Athenian citizens sent their sons to school at the age of seven. Although schooling had to be paid for, it was not very expensive and most boys would have had at least a few years' education. There were three main subjects: literature, physical education and music. Literature included reading, writing, grammar and learning poetry, particularly Homer, by heart.

Craftwork

The central area of the city, around the marketplace, was crowded with workshops where craftspeople worked iron and bronze, and made shoes, bags, pots, jewelry and other items. Most workshops were family-owned businesses with just a few people working in them. They sold their products one by one to the public who dropped by their premises, or bargained with merchants who took larger quantities to sell to clients in the local shops or for export.

Clothing

Both men and women wore simple tunics, known as *chitons*, made from wool or linen. They were made from two squares of cloth sewn together down the sides. They were often held at the waist by a belt or girdle so that they fell in soft pleats. In the winter they wore thick cloaks, called *himations*, over their tunics.

Scene from a vase painting showing a cobbler's workshop. Sandals and shoes could be made to measure.

Right: Two examples of some quite elaborate leather sandals. The Greeks wore a range of different kinds of shoes, including sandals, full shoes and pull-on or lace-up boots.

The agora

The agora was an open space in the city center where citizens could meet. It was filled with stalls selling goods and surrounded by temples, shops, workshops and public buildings. Most men spent a part of each day in the agora talking to friends and discussing politics.

Scene in a blacksmith's workshop. The figure on the right is holding a piece of heated metal with tongs. The figure on the right is about to beat it into shape using an ax. A selection of tools is hanging on the wall behind.

Three official measures, found in the agora at Athens.

Weights and measures

Official weights and measures were used for both dry and wet goods. Stamped with official marks, they came in varying sizes and shapes according to their use. Everyone used the same ones so that weights and measures were standardized. There were penalties for anyone who tried to give short measure.

Many coins from Athens had images of owls on them. It was one of the symbols of the city.

Sparta

The government and social organization of Sparta was unique among ancient Greek states. It was ruled by two lifetime kings, who had total power during wartime and only slightly less during times of peace, when they shared the task of ruling Sparta with a senate of 30 male citizens. In the 8th century BCE Sparta developed a strong army and soon conquered its neighbors, whose citizens (known as "helots" by the Spartans) were kept almost in a state of slavery. Because the Spartans were outnumbered by their "subjects" by about seven to one, they were forced to maintain a powerful military and a rigid social order. All male citizens joined the army at five years of age and they stayed in it until they were thirty.

This clay head of a warrior was made near Sparta in about 700 BCE.

Spartan war helmet, probably of an aristocratic soldier. Spartan society was based on a military hierarchy of soldier castes, unified by a fierce discipline.

Spartan vase showing two wrestling scenes. In the larger scene, the man on the left has blood pouring from his nose, but the fight continues.

The origins of Sparta

According to legend, Sparta was founded in the 9th century BCE, although there are few records from this very early period. During the 8th century BCE the Spartans conquered neighboring Messenia, a land that was "good to plow and good to hoe" (in the words of the Spartan poet Tyrtaeus). This was a turning point for Sparta, which from then on needed a strong army to subdue its large subject population. State land was allotted to citizens and the conquered heliots worked on it, giving a half of what they produced to their rulers.

This Athenian vase painting shows Helen, wife of the Spartan king, Meneleus, with Priam, king of Troy. According to Greek legend, the Trojan war broke out when Priam's son Paris kidnapped Helen and took her back to his homeland.

Bust of the Spartan military commander Pausanias, who led the combined Greek army to victory against the Persians in the Persian Wars. He was later accused of treason and then suspected of plotting an uprising against Sparta. He sought refuge in a temple that the Spartans walled up while he was still inside. He starved to death in the temple.

The Peloponnesian War (431–404 BCE)

Sparta and Athens were the most powerful city-states in ancient Greece. They each commanded alliances of other states and between them they controlled almost the entire Greek world. When war broke out between the two in 431 BCE, it was brutal and devastating. The Athenians, who had many overseas colonies, were richer and commanded a powerful navy. The Spartans, however, could count on their well-trained army. The war, which involved costly battles (many as far away as southern Italy), dragged on until 405 BCE when the Athenian fleet was finally destroyed by the Spartans. Athens itself surrendered the following year.

Athens

Sparta

Aegean Sea

The vase of Vix

This large bronze vase was found in the grave of a Celtic princess just south of Paris, France. However, it was clearly made by a Greek artisan working in Sparta in the late 6th century BCE. The detail reproduced above is taken from the neck of the vase that shows seven ferocious

Spartan warriors and seven war chariots. The foot soldier (1) is nude except for his elaborate helmet (2) and large shield (3). Four sturdy horses (4) are pulling the lightweight war chariot carrying the second warrior (5). The artist has skillfully captured all the ominous power that Spartan warriors were widely believed to inspire.

Below: The vase of Vix.

Spartan women

Greek women did not enjoy very much personal freedom. In wealthy households the women's quarters were separate from the main part of the house. Respectable women were not allowed to leave the house without a male companion. Girls generally were not sent to school, nor did they take part in physical training in most parts of Greece. Only in Sparta do records show that girls were allowed to train as athletes and take part in some sporting events. Spartan women may have enjoyed more freedom and power in other areas of life as well.

Tiny votive statues from the sanctuary of Artemis at Sparta of a man playing the double pipes (right) and a warrior in full armor (left).

Colonies and Trade

Between the 8th and 6th centuries BCE the Greek city-states founded colonies in many parts of the Mediterranean and around the shores of the Black Sea. Founding a colony was a formal undertaking; a leader was chosen, magistrates were appointed who would parcel out the land in the new colony, and an oracle was consulted to choose the best time and place. Surprisingly, the new colonies were independent of their founding cities from the outset. The settlers themselves never returned to their homelands, although some contact was maintained through trade. The colonists spread the Greek language and ways everywhere they settled. The Greek influence was spread even farther afield through the extensive trade routes they developed.

The Greeks founded several colonies on the coast of Thrace (modern Bulgaria), the most important of which was Constantinople (modern Istanbul). The silver rhyton (drinking horn), left, made in Thrace during the 4th century BCE, shows a mixture of Greek and Thracian elements.

This 4th-century BCE Phoenician glass vase was found on the Mediterranean island of Sardinia, the southern part of which was a Phoenician colony.

The Phoenicians

The ancient land of Phoenicia lay in the Levant, where Lebanon is today. The Phoenicians were excellent sea-traders and colonizers. By the time the Greeks began to colonize the Mediterranean, the Phoenicians already controlled the coasts of North Africa and much of Spain. Although rivals, the two powers traded and also exchanged ideas. For example, the Greek alphabet is based on the much earlier Phoenician one.

Reconstruction of a vase-maker's house at Locri, in southern Italy. Pottery amphorae (jars), vases, jugs and containers of every sort were in high demand for transporting and storing oil, wine and water.

Jars going off to be sold

Well

Finished jars

Kiln

Clay statue of a youth on horseback from a temple at Locri, southern Italy. The horse is resting on a sphinx.

Magna Grecia

There were so many Greek colonies in southern Italy and Sicily that the area became known as *Magna Grecia* (Greater Greece). The region's closeness to Greece, its good farmland and many natural harbors made it an obvious choice for settlement. Colonies were limited to the south because of the powerful Etruscan civilization that controlled central Italy at the time (although there was frequent contact between the two). The Romans absorbed much of what they knew of Greek culture from the southern colonies.

Painted statue of the gorgon, Medusa, from the altar of a temple at Syracuse, Sicily. In Greek mythology Medusa was one of three monsters. She was always shown as a winged figure with a round face and with her tongue hanging out of her mouth. Here she is clutching her son, the winged horse Pegasus.

Legend

- Phoenicia
- Phoenician colonies
- Greek homelands
- Greek colonies
- Etruscan states
- Tin route to Cornwell
- Phoenician trade routes
- Greek trade routes

CORNWALL

SPAIN

ETRURIA

Black Sea

NORTH AFRICA

MAGNA GRAECIA

GREECE

ANATOLIA

CRETE

Mediterranean Sea

Colonies and trade

The map shows the main colonies and trade routes around the Mediterranean and Black seas from about 800–500 BCE. The Greeks are mainly concentrated in southern Italy and France and in the Black Sea area. The Phoenicians control the Levant and much of North Africa and southern Spain.

Bronze griffin from a wine bowl. The griffin is a typically eastern motif. It was made in a Greek city in Asia Minor in around 650 BCE.

Illustration of the Nereid Monument as reconstructed in the British Museum. Built in the form of a small Ionic temple (originally at Lycia in Asia Minor), it shows a mixture of Greek and Persian attributes.

The Black Sea colonies

During the 8th century Greek colonizing efforts were concentrated mainly on Italy. During the 7th and 6th centuries they concentrated more on Thrace and the Black Sea regions. The Greek colonies in these areas traded Greek-made luxury goods with the people of the steppes for wheat to feed the cities in the Greek homeland. Colonies in North Africa (Cyrenaica and Egypt) were also founded at about this time.

Statue of the Greek goddess Aphrodite, made by the Bactrian people in central Asia. The Greek influence spread far beyond the colonies themselves.

The Near East

By 900 BCE the coastal areas of Anatolia and the island of Rhodes were part of Greece itself. One of the first colonies in the Near East was founded at Al Mina, in Syria. The Persians and the Egyptians only allowed the Greeks to set up small trading colonies in the areas they controlled. The colony at Al Mina, for example, stood at the head of an overland route to Mesopotamia.

This vase painting shows a wild boar being caught. Hunting was a popular sport among wealthy Greeks. Wild boars, deer and hares were common catches. However, hunting was always more of a sport than a main source of meat. Fishing, on the other hand, was widely practiced and fish were an important source of protein in the Greek diet.

Below: Bronze statue of an African slave. There were thousands of slaves in ancient Greece and almost every household owned at least one. Wealthy families could own as many as fifty.

Skillful Greek craftspeople made beautiful pottery vases, many of which were painted with mythological scenes. They also made intricate jewelry and art objects.

What was traded

Generally speaking, the cities of mainland Greece imported basic necessities, such as cereals, olive oil, wine and salt-fish, from their colonies and from neighboring countries. They paid for these goods with luxury items, including pottery, jewelry and other craftwork. Other commonly traded goods included timber, minerals, slaves, marble and glass.

Vase showing farmers harvesting the olives by shaking them out of the trees using long sticks.

Farming

The hilly Greek countryside, combined with its hot, dry summers and cold winters, does not make Greece an ideal place for farming. Only about 20 percent of the land was suitable for growing vegetables, wheat and other cereals. The lower slopes of the hills were used to grow olives and grapes. Even so, agriculture formed the basis of the Greek economy. Most farms were small, family-run operations.

As the populations of the cities of mainland Greece increased, so did the need for basic foodstuffs. Records from Athens show that the city was dependent upon the arrival of wheat in the city port of Piraeus. The local government passed laws forcing merchants to land their goods there.

Painted plate from Cyrene

This painting shows King Arkesilas II (1), of the Greek colony of Cyrene (in modern Libya), scepter in hand (2), as he oversees a bustling trading scene. Some of his servants (2) are carrying sacks (probably of dried herbs, for which the colony was famous) to be weighed, while others appear to be filling up sacks and taking note of weights (3). The merchandise was probably being prepared for export to the Greek mainland. The scales are held in place by a stork (4) and other animals. The leopard cub (5), lizard (6) and monkey (7), all typically African animals, remind us where the scene is taking place.

Money

Metal coins began to be used to pay for goods during the 7th century BCE in Anatolia (modern Turkey). Their use spread quickly throughout the Greek world. Each city-state minted its own coins, decorated with local designs, such as the heads of rulers or local products.

Trade and commerce

Small merchants operated from the craft workshops near the central marketplace. As trade developed, larger merchants began to operate in the ports, where they offered ships for hire and generally controlled imports and exports. Many became very rich, not just from trading but also from loaning money to other traders (often at very high interest rates).

Scene from a vase painting showing a sleek pirate galley speeding after a merchant ship. Piracy was a problem and some city-states sent their merchant fleets out in groups protected by the navy.

War

The Greek city-states were often at war among themselves. The Peloponnesian War (431–404 BCE), which involved almost all the city-states under either the Athenian or Spartan banners, was the worst internal clash. Earlier in the same century, the city-states had banded together to fight off the Persians when they tried to invade. The Greeks won the Persian Wars (490–479 BCE) against all odds. Although outnumbered at the famous battles of Marathon and Salamis, they won them both through a combination of skillful tactics, bravery and good fortune. During the 4th century BCE, a Greek warrior – Alexander the Great – forged one of the largest empires the world has ever known.

Battle scene from a vase showing Achilles killing the Amazon queen Penthesilea at Troy. It shows how fearsome the Greek warriors must have looked in their armor and plumed helmets.

Helmet styles changed greatly depending on the period and region. The helmet above has the typical narrow eye sockets and overlapping noseguard of the Corinthian style while the one on the right is typical of Sparta.

This diagram shows the way the rowers in the trireme were seated on three different levels. They were given their stroke by a piper, whose pulsating notes could be heard above the roar of the battle.

Warships

The trireme became the mainstay of the Greek navy from the 5th century BCE onward. Each of the sleek vessels was powered into battle by 170 rowers. There were only a handful of soldiers aboard, since the object was not to board enemy ships but to build up enough speed to smash into them with the metal-tipped ram at the front. At its height, Athens commanded a fleet of 400 triremes.

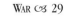

Greek foot soldiers in battle

This painting on a 7th-century BCE vase, made at Corinth, shows hoplites (foot soldiers)

engaged in battle. They are all carrying long lances (1) and brightly painted shields (2), and wearing protective breastplate armor (3), plumed helmets (4) and greaves to protect their knees and shins (5). To the left (6) a piper is playing flute music while they fight.

The diagram below shows a phalanx of Greek soldiers ready to attack the enemy. This was a typical formation, with row upon row of armored warriors pouring forth. When the soldier in the front line got hit and fell to the ground his place was immediately taken by the one behind. This meant that the ranks were never broken.

Reconstruction of a Greek warrior in full battle gear.

Weapons and tactics

Soldiers in the Classical period were usually armed with long lances, but they often had throwing spears, arrows, slings and swords, too. Up until the 5th century BCE, most soldiers were citizens of the city-state they fought for. As such, they were expected to supply their own armor and weapons and richer men had to bring their own horses. Paid armies of professional soldiers developed during the Peloponnesian War in the 5th century.

Entertainment

Wealthy, city-dwelling Greeks had plenty of leisure time and there was a wide variety of activities they could take part in, either as participants or spectators. Public entertainment included theater, poetry readings accompanied by music, dancing and sporting events. At home men enjoyed evening banquets and drinking parties, where they discussed philosophy and politics (and probably gossiped as well). Dancing and music was provided by actors and musicians. Respectable women, who lived fairly secluded lives, also had their parties and dinners, although we know less about them. Children had toys and games and pets, much as they do today.

Symposiums and drinking parties

Greek men liked to dine in the company of friends in the evenings and they held dinner parties, which were called symposiums. The guests arrived at dusk and began with dinner. Depending on how wealthy their host was, they would eat a meal of fish, oysters and other seafood, bread, cheese, poultry, meat, some vegetables and olives. The guests' hands were then washed and fruit was brought in for dessert. Wine was served throughout the meal. Afterward the tables were cleared and the drinking party began. The guests talked, played games, recited poetry and were entertained by professional musicians and dancers.

This vase, painted by the famous vase painter, Exekias, shows the Greek heroes Ajax and Achilles playing drafts.

Chariot racing was a very popular sport and the winners enjoyed enormous prestige. It was a sport for the wealthy, since the chariot and horses were expensive. Sometimes professional charioteers were used.

Athletes competed in the nude. These men are running what must be a sprint, since their pumping hands and legs suggest speed rather than the endurance required for marathons.

Sports

Sports were perhaps the most highly regarded form of entertainment and the Greeks took them seriously. Young men were expected to train every day to develop their fitness and physical attractiveness. A well-proportioned body was considered the outward sign of a developed mind. The most common sports were running, long jump, wrestling, discus, javelin throwing, boxing and horse racing. In most places women were not permitted to take part in sporting events. Sparta seems to have been the exception to this and records show women athletes competing there.

Statue of a boxer resting, from the 1st century BCE. His hands, wrapped with "gloves," and the open wounds on his face show just how violent this sport could be.

Vase painting with a theater scene

This 4th-century BCE vase shows a scene from a comedy. In Greek theater there were normally only three actors on the stage at once (all men, even if they were dressed as women). In this case, a circus acrobat (1), standing on his hands, and a comic actor, wearing a very ugly mask (2), are facing toward the seated figure of an actor representing Dionysos (3). Above, to the left and right of the acrobat, two female theatrical masks (4) are framed in the windows. All actors wore masks the whole time they were on stage.

Toys and games

Children played with spinning tops, knucklebones (like the girl shown at left), wooden and clay toys, rattles and dolls. They also had board games, such as snakes and ladders and drafts. Many children also kept pets, including cats, dogs, hens, ducks, monkeys and tortoises.

These painted clay figures were children's toys.

A teacher instructing two youths how to play the lyre.

Theater

The Greeks enjoyed going to the theater, probably because the plays they saw were so good. Many of the works that have survived from Classical times are still considered some of the greatest ever written and they are still performed today. Plays were put on in steep-sided, open-air theaters. Sometimes, as in the great spring festival in Athens – the City Dionysia – spectators sat from dawn until dusk for four consecutive days watching the latest plays by the best dramatists.

Music

Music was the constant companion of most activities in ancient Greece, not only the obvious ones like dancing or at banquets and feast days, but also during war, athletic competitions and everyday tasks, such as baking bread. Boys were taught to play instruments and sing at school.

Learning music and song was thought to have a civilizing effect on *"the boys' minds, to make them less wild, and better in tune for effective discourse and action."*

Sculpted head of the first great Athenian playwright Aeschylus. His most famous works include Agamemnon, The Furies *and* Prometheus Bound.

The Alexander mosaic

This huge Roman mosaic (it measures almost 20 ft by 10 ft, or 6 m by 3 m) is a copy of an earlier Greek painting. It celebrates Alexander the Great's victory over the Persian king, Darius III. Both leaders are clearly visible: Alexander on the left (1), mounted on horseback and without a helmet, and Darius on the right (2), on a retreating war chariot and wearing a helmet. Battle rages all around them. In the center foreground a horse has fallen (3) and his rider is picking himself up as Alexander bears down on him, stabbing him with his long lance (4). Behind Darius, to the left and right, long lances point skyward. (5).

This 4th-century BCE lion mosaic comes from the royal palace of Pella, home to the kings of Macedonia. Lion hunting, a sport imported from the Near East, was a favorite pastime for Macedonian kings and also a common motif for artists.

The Hellenistic Period

The Hellenistic period (336–31 BCE) covers the 300 years or so between the reign of Alexander the Great and the rise of the first Roman Emperor, Augustus. This was the time in which Greek culture, although weakened at home, spread across western Asia, as far east as northern India. Alexander the Great conquered a vast empire that split into three main kingdoms on his death in 323 BCE. These kingdoms were: the Macedonian (Alexander's homeland, north of Greece), the Seleucid (from Anatolia to Persia), and the Ptolemaic (in Egypt). Although there were frequent wars between the three, the Greek language and culture united the region. It was a highly creative time, at least until about 160 BCE, when the growing power of Rome began to cast its shadow over the Greek world.

Marble head of a youthful Alexander, attributed to the Greek sculptor Leochares.

Alexander the Great

Alexander III of Macedonia was born in Pella in 356 BCE. He came to the throne just 20 years later when his father was murdered. Alexander quickly consolidated his power at home and then set off on a journey of conquest that took him as far east as India. His empire, which stretched for over 20,000 miles (32,187 km), remained under Greek control until the Romans took over 300 years later.

This dynamic bronze statue of Alexander the Great on a rearing horse (probably his favorite, Bucephalus) was made in Roman times. Of all the portraits, it best catches the spirit of Alexander's life.

Aristotle

One of the two greatest Greek philosophers, Aristotle (384–322 BCE) grew up at the royal court of Macedonia, where his father was a doctor. When his father died, he was sent to Athens to study under the other great philosopher, Plato. In 342 BCE Aristotle returned to the Macedonian court where he was tutor to the young Alexander for three years. On returning to Athens he founded an important school. Aristotle's writings deal with every branch of human knowledge. They have influenced both Western and Muslim thought greatly over the centuries.

Coin with the head of Ptolemy I of Egypt (364–283 BCE).

Alexandria

Alexander the Great founded the Egyptian city of Alexandria in 332 BCE. It became the capital of his new Egyptian dominion and the base for his navy. When Alexander died, Ptolemy took power and founded a dynasty in his name. Within a century of its founding, Alexandria became the greatest city in the world and a center of Greek learning. The largest Greek library in antiquity, containing almost 500,000 book rolls, was kept in the city. The library was destroyed during a civil war in the 3rd century CE.

Hellenist art and science

The Hellenist age was an inventive time, both in the fields of art and science. Works of art became more expressive and some of the best-known pieces of Greek art, including the *Venus de Milo* and the *Laocoon* group, date to this time. The great mathematician Euclid, best-known for his treaty on geometry, lived during the Hellenistic period. Advances were also made in technology.

Reconstruction of the lighthouse of Alexandria, which stood in the ancient quarter of Pharos. It was considered one of the Seven Wonders of World.

The Greek Influence

Greek culture and ideas have probably influenced subsequent societies, particularly in Europe and America, more than those of any other ancient civilization. The Romans, who conquered what remained of Alexander the Great's empire, were the first of many to borrow from Greek institutions and ideas. During the Renaissance, in 14th- to 16th-century Europe, there was a huge revival of interest in Greek and Roman art, literature and thought. Greek influence has continued right up to the present. It is difficult to think of an area of modern life that has not been touched by the Greeks—from the Greek alphabet, which lies at the basis of most written languages in the West, to political concepts (such as democracy) and modern science and medicine, not to mention the fields of sport (including the Olympic Games), art and philosophy.

The English poet Lord Byron was one of many artists of the 19th-century Romantic era who were inspired by ancient Greece. Byron was so impressed by the Greek heritage that he joined the fight to liberate Greece from the Turks. While in Greece, he caught a fever and died at just 36 years of age.

Diagram of an atom. In the 5th century BCE, Greek thinkers proposed that all things in nature were made up of basic particles, which they called "atoms." As in many other areas of scientific thought, modern science has shown that, substantially, the Greeks were right.

The Villa Rotunda, near Vicenza, Italy, was built by the famous 16th-century architect Andrea Palladio. Palladio modelled his work on the Roman architect Vitruvius, who in turn was strongly influenced by the Greeks.

This bronze statue by Renaissance artist Benvenuto Cellini is called Ganymede and the Eagle. *It shows the Greek hero Ganymede who, according to legend, was so handsome that he was carried off by the gods to become a cupbearer.*

Art, architecture and literature

It is hard to overstate the importance of the Greeks in these fields. The Romans adopted many Greek ideas in their literature and art, and together the impact of "Classical" (Greek and Roman) thought has shaped them ever since.

This athlete is carrying the Olympic flame. Every time the games are held the flame is carried all the way from Olympia, Greece, to celebrate the opening ceremony.

The painted plate below shows the Three Graces. This subject, found in Roman art, was derived from the Greeks. It became very popular again during the Renaissance.

The Capitol in Washington, D.C., is built in the Classical style.

The Olympic Games

The first Olympics took place at Olympia, Greece, in 776 BCE. They were held at four-year intervals after that until they were suppressed by the Roman Emperor Theodosius I, in 393 CE. The Games were revived again in 1896 by the French Baron Pierre de Coubertin. They have been held once every four years since that time (except during the two World Wars in the 20th century).

Politics

The ideal of democracy, which means rule by the people, was first invented by the Greeks. Although 5th-century BCE Athens, with its many slaves and non-citizens, would not be considered democratic by today's standards, this was where the idea of all citizens having a say in how their society was run came from.

Below: Head of Hippocrates. The Hippocratic Oath, *a code of conduct for doctors, has guided the practice of medicine in the West for more than 2,000 years.*

The Rape of Europa

This painting (left) by the eighteenth century French artist Sebastien Leclerc (le Jeune, or the Younger) illustrates a famous Greek myth. In this myth, Europa, the daughter of Phoenix, king of Phoenicia, was so beautiful that Zeus decided to kidnap her. Zeus appeared in the form of a white bull. At first he was very nice to her, and she garlanded his horns with flowers. When he told her to climb on his back, her attendants helped her up. Then the bull ran toward the sea and finally disappeared with Europa on his back. The painter Leclerc was best known for paintings on historical, mythological, and biblical subjects.

Science and medicine

Greek thinkers based their knowledge on direct observation of the world. Many of the ideas we take for granted today, such as the link between disease and natural (rather than supernatural) causes, were first proposed by the Greeks.

Glossary

agora In ancient Greece, a place of assembly, often the marketplace.

antiquity The early period of history, before the Middle Ages; the quality of being ancient or old.

archaic Belonging to an earlier period; ancient.

aristocratic Characteristic of the upper class, the ruling minority of elites.

chaperon An older person who accompanies younger people in public or at social gatherings, like parties and dances, in order to supervise their behavior.

citizen A native or inhabitant of a place, such as a city, state or country; a member of a state or nation who swears allegiance to it and who enjoys full civil rights.

city-state A state made up of an independent city and the territory directly controlled by it.

civilization A social organization of high order, marked by the development and use of a written language and advances in the arts, sciences and government.

colony A group of people who settle in a distant land but remain under the political control of their native land; a territory distant from the state that controls it.

deity A god or goddess.

dominion The power and authority to rule over something or someone, such as conquered peoples, a state, nation or empire.

elaborate Worked out carefully; developed in great detail; highly ornamented; complicated.

empire A group of states, territories and/or peoples governed by an absolute ruler, such as an emperor.

export To send goods to another country in order to sell them.

foundry A place where metal is melted and molded.

fresco A painting made by applying watercolors on wet plaster.

frieze A decoration, often featuring sculpture, forming an ornamental band around a room or mantel.

hoplite A heavily armed foot soldier of ancient Greece.

import To bring in goods from another country in order to sell them domestically (in the home country).

intellectual A member of the educated classes whose primary occupation involves the use of the intellect through literary, philosophical, theoretical, political or other high-level cultural pursuits.

libation The act of pouring out wine or oil onto the ground as a sacrifice to a god.

lyre A small stringed instrument of the harp family, used by the ancient Greeks to accompany singers and reciters.

magistrate A civil officer empowered to administer and enforce the law.

migration A group of people (or animals or birds) moving from one place to another.

mourner A person who is expressing grief and sorrow, usually for someone who has died.

oracle A place where deities are consulted, a person believed to be in communication with a deity, and/or the opinions expressed by the deity through this person.

procession A number of persons or things moving forward, as in a parade, in an orderly, formal way.

ritual A set form or system of rites, religious or otherwise; the observance of set forms or rites, such as in public worship.

sacrifice The act of offering the life of a person or animal or some object in honor of a god.

sanctuary A holy place; a building set aside for worship of a god or gods.

steppe Any of the great plains of southeast Europe and Asia.

symposium A meeting or social gathering in which ideas are freely exchanged, discussed and/or debated.

tunic A loose, gown-like garment worn by men and women in ancient Greece.

For More Information

Acropolis Museum
15 Dionysiou Areopagitou Street
Athens 11742, Greece
Tel.: +30 210 9000900
Web site: http://www.theacropolismuseum.gr
The Acropolis Museum is an archaeological museum focused on the findings of the archaeological site of the Acropolis of Athens. The museum was built in order to house every artifact found on the rock and on its feet, covering a large period of time, from the Greek Bronze Age to Roman and Byzantine Greece.

British Museum
Department of Greek and Roman Antiquities
Great Russell Street
London, England WC1B 3DG
Telephone: +44 (0)20 7323 8321
Web site: http://www.britishmuseum.org/the_museum/departments/greek_and_roman_antiquities.aspx
The Department of Greece and Rome at the British Museum has one of the most comprehensive collections of antiquities from the Classical world, with over 100,000 objects. These mostly range in date from the beginning of the Greek Bronze Age (about 3200 BCE) to the reign of the Roman emperor Constantine in the 4th century CE.

Center for Hellenic Studies
3100 Whitehaven Street NW
Washington, DC 20008
(202) 745-4400
Web site: http://chs.harvard.edu/chs/chs_home
The Center for Hellenic Studies (CHS) is a research institute located in Washington, D.C., that is affiliated with Harvard University. Its mission is to bring together a variety of research and teaching interests centering on Hellenic civilization and a re-discovery of the humanism of the Hellenic Greeks.

Metropolitan Museum of Art

Department of Greek and Roman Art

1000 Fifth Avenue

New York, NY 10028-0198

(212) 535-7710

Web site: http://www.metmuseum.org/Works_of_Art/greek_and_roman_art

The collection of Greek and Roman art at the Metropolitan Museum—more than 17,000 works ranging in date from the Neolithic period to the time of the Roman emperor Constantine's conversion to Christianity in 312 CE—includes the art of many cultures and is among the most comprehensive in North America.

Nicholas P. Goulandris Foundation—Museum of Cycladic Art

4, Neophytou Douka str.

Athens 106 74, Greece

Telephone: (+30) 210 7228321-3

Web site: http://www.cycladic.gr/frontoffice/portal.asp?cpage=NODE&cnode=1

The Museum of Cycladic Art is dedicated to the study and promotion of ancient cultures of the Aegean and Cyprus, with special emphasis on Cycladic Art of the 3rd millennium BCE. Today, in the galleries of the MCA, the visitor can approach three major subjects: the Cycladic Culture of the Early Bronze Age (3200–2000 BCE); the Ancient Greek Art, from the Bronze Age to Late Roman times (2nd millenium BCE–4th century CE); and the Cypriot Culture from the Chalcolithic Age to the Early Christian period (4th millenium BCE–6th century CE).

Web Sites

Due to the changing nature of Internet links, Rosen Publishing has developed an online list of Web sites related to the subject of this book. This site is updated regularly. Please use this link to access this list:

http://www.rosenlinks.com/aac/gree

For Further Reading

Adkins, Lesley, and Roy A. Adkins. *Handbook to Life in Ancient Greece*. New York, NY: Facts On File, 2005.

Chisolm, Jane, Lisa Miles, and Struan Reid. *Encyclopedia of Ancient Greece*. Eveleth, MN: Usborne Books, 2007.

DK Publishing. *Ancient Greece* (Eyewitness Workbooks). New York, NY: DK Children, 2008.

Haaren, John H., and A. B. Poland. *Famous Men of Greece*. Chapel Hill, NC: Yesterday's Classics, 2006.

Osborne, Mary Pope, and Natalie Pope Boyce. *Ancient Greece and the Olympics* (Magic Tree House Research Guide).
   New York, NY: Random House Books for Young Readers, 2004.

Pearson, Anne. *Ancient Greece* (DK Eyewitness Books). New York, NY: DK Children, 2007.

Powell, Anton. *Ancient Greece* (Cultural Atlas for Young People). New York, NY: Chelsea House Publishers, 2007.

Tames, Richard. *Ancient Greece* (Passport to the Past). New York, NY: Rosen Publishing Group, Inc., 2009.

Weber, Belinda. *The Best Book of Ancient Greece*. New York, NY: Kingfisher, 2005.

Index

About the Author

Dimitra Tsakiridis lives in Philadelphia, Pennsylvania.

*The publishers would like to thank the following picture libraries and photographers for permission
to reproduce their photos:*

Cover (right, top to bottom): © www.istockphoto.com/Constantinos Gerakis, © www.istockphoto.com/Marco Testa,
© www.istockphoto.com/Serdar Yagci, © www.istockphoto.com/Asher Welstead

7 Scala Group, Florence; 9 Scala Group, Florence; 15 Scala Group, Florence; 19 Corbis-Grazia Neri; 29 Scala Group, Florence;
31 Scala Group, Florence; 32 Scala Group, Florence; 34 Réunion des Musées Nationaux/Art Resource, NY.